SUMMARY

OF

WHAT TO EAT WHEN:

A strategic Plan to Improve Your Health
and Life Through Food

MICHAEL ROIZEN & MICHAEL CRUPAIN

High Speed Reads

10683790

TABLE OF CONTENTS

THIRTY SECOND SUMMARY

Doctors and authors Michael Roizen, chief wellness officer at the Cleveland Clinic and Michael Crupain, multiple Emmy Award-winning producer and medical unit chief of staff for *The Dr. Oz Show*, join forces with Ted Spiker, former articles editor for *Men's Health* to bring readers *What to Eat When*. This book serves as a roadmap to healthy eating like no other. While many diet books may focus solely on food, this book explores the *when* as well as the *what* aspects of eating. This diet plan, dubbed the When Way, guides readers through when to eat and in what circumstance. From vacation to the holidays, *What to Eat When* will guide you through the ins and outs of healthy eating no matter the situation.

PART 1: HOW FOOD WORKS

CHAPTER 1: THE SCIENCE OF WHEN

SUMMARY

Our lives are often dictated by time and "good timing," and we should consider a similar approach when we're looking at health. *What* we eat and *when* we eat are equally important. Our bodies are complicated ecosystems that require both appropriate timing and fuel. This *timing* must occur on two different levels. The first of these must take into consideration our bodies' changing states; we experience differences in emotions, fluctuations in hormones, and different states of health. Therefore, we must learn to adapt what we eat to these situations. This timing also depends on the time of day, a twenty-four hour cycle, and how eating affects our performance.

Circadian Rhythm 101

Most diets focus on what food is best to eat. Some may also focus on *when*, while other diets argue that *when* doesn't matter. While most diets can find some common ground, as in what food is or isn't healthy, the topic of *when* and its importance varies. But *when* is the key to eating healthy. Food should be considered within the context of your circadian rhythm, your individual biological clock.

Human beings evolved for instinctually saving energy, which helped survival. Our circadian rhythm, operating from day-to-day, is one of these instincts. This rhythm sends hormones through our bodies, telling us when to eat and sleep. Because our bodies are made for efficiency, your circadian rhythm tries not to waste energy. However, some of us may not follow our natural rhythms. We might, for example, work night shifts, and this is where food comes into play.

Circadian Rhythm and Your Food Clock

Your internal clock affects you every day, from when you want to sleep to when you need to eat. The trick is to snyc your *circadian rhythm* with your internal *food clock*. The problem is that, while human beings want to eat most at night, we do better when we have food earlier in the day. Once an evolutionary advantage, this may hurt us now. This is further complicated by your organs, which have their own clocks that may impact when you want to eat.

Insulin is one of the most crucial hormones when dealing with food, and studies indicate humans are more resistant to insulin as the day progresses. When you eat affects your blood sugar, which—in turn—means your body is keyed to eat at certain times. To be healthiest, we need to eat earlier in the day rather than later.

The Microbiome's Circadian Rhythm

The bacteria in our gut compose a microbiome, and in this case, we want a very diverse ecosystem of bacteria. Fortunately, we can increase this diversity by tinkering with what and when we eat. This is another reason that it's better to eat earlier in the day.

Recap of Chapter 1

- To eat healthy, looking at *when* we eat is just as important as *what* we eat.
- Our body has a natural rhythm, our circadian clock, that we must align with our internal food clock.
- For best results, we should eat more early in that day rather than later.

CHAPTER 2: A NUTRITIOUS BREAKDOWN

SUMMARY

For good health, it is crucial to have an understanding of how food works within your body. Not knowing how food works and how it impacts your body is a recipe for disaster. Part of understanding food is in knowing about the three major macronutrients and the ways in which these work inside your body.

The Macronutrients: Power and Effects

Food provides your body with energy, and this energy comes from three primary macronutrients; carbohydrates and fat, responsible for providing energy, and proteins, responsible for building your body. These three components are called *macro*nutrients because our bodies need a lot of them to be healthy. Additionally, our bodies need micronutrients—vitamins, minerals, etc.—and together, the macro- and micronutrients help our bodies function to their fullest potential.

Carbohydrates

You've probably heard a lot, both good and bad, about carbohydrates, but these are simply sugars. There are many types of sugars in chemistry, but the main ones we consume are divided into simple sugar, starch, and fiber. These sugar molecules break down into glucose, which provides our bodies with energy. Glucose is converted to glycogen, which acts as reserved energy inside our bodies. While carbohydrates are important, though, not all carbohydrates are created equal. Complex carbo-hydrates—for example, grains and fiber—do your body more good than simple sugars—like white flour and table sugar. Be-cause of this, so-called "white carbs," most often found in pro-cessed foods, should be consumed more sparingly than whole grains, fruits, and vegetables.

Fat

For years, we thought that eating fat equaled a larger waist-line, but we have since learned this is not entirely true. Fat, which can be used for long-term energy, comes in two varieties: saturated and unsaturated. The primary difference is that satu-rated fat usually comes from animal products, while unsaturated fats come from plants. Of the two, unsaturated fats are better, some varieties even carrying major health benefits.

Unsaturated fats come in two kinds—monounsaturated and polyunsaturated. Monounsaturated fats, come from foods like olive oil, avocadoes, and most nuts. A diet rich in Monounsatu-rated fats is known to be associated with less of the worst type of fat, visceral fat. polyunsaturated fats, which includes fatty oils found in fish, are good for you and can reduce risk for heart dis-ease.

Trans Fat

Trans fats are the worst fats. In fact, their risks are so great that the FDA has banned them in foods. It is expected that all products containing trans fats will be off the shelves by 2020. However, this fat does naturally occur in some foods, such as milk, pork, and beef; because of this, those foods are not recom-mended.

Protein

While protein can be used for energy after it's been converted into glucose, it functions primarily as a building block for your body. Proteins are composed of amino acids, which help your body function. While high-protein diets are very en vogue, the body doesn't need more than 82 grams, or approximately 10 oz. of grilled chicken breast, a day. Too much protein can also lead to health problems.

The Digestive Process and the Blood Sugar Problem

As food passes through your body, it is broken down, and the way it's broken down and its impact depends on what you're eating. For example, carbohydrates are important, and when you eat them, your blood sugar goes up. If your blood sugar goes up *too high*, it causes serious problems. You can develop diabetes or even insulin resistance, and again, timing is important. Because our bodies are more resistant to insulin during the night, we're more likely to raise our blood sugar if we eat large meals late in the day.

Too much of any of the macronutrients is not good for you and can cause weight gain. While we tend to think of fat as being simply under the skin, there is another fat which forms around our organs, and this fat—visceral fat—is much more dangerous. It can cause serious health problems. To find out if you have too much of this fat, you can measure your ratios. A healthy person should have a waist that is half or less than your height. For this measurement, you can even suck in your stomach! We're looking at the fat that's inside.

And fear not! One way to lose this weight is knowing *when* to eat.

Recap of chapter 2

1. Our bodies require three macronutrients—carbohy-drates, fats, and proteins—to function.
2. The key to being healthy is to know the effects that mac-ronutrients have on our body; all these macronutrients are crucial to our health, but too much of any one can have adverse effects.
3. Unhealthy eating can cause the gain of dangerous vis-ceral fat, which can be lost by mastering *when* to eat.

PART 2: THE WHEN WAY

CHAPTER 3: TIME TO EAT!

SUMMARY

The best way to eat is in knowing how to adjust what you eat. While there are a lot of misconceptions for how to do this, we've narrowed it down to four guidelines.

Guideline 1: Eat When the Sun Shines

This goes back to *when* you eat. It's best to eat during the day, preferably during a window of less than twelve hours. It's also best to make the time you eat match the time when you're hungry. This aligns with our bodies' natural rhythms. Slowly, try eating during this twelve-hour window during the day for three days and work your way up to longer times.

Guideline 2: Eat More in the Morning and Less Later On

It is best to front-load your food and eat earlier in the day rather than later. It's a cliché, but breakfast truly is the most important meal of the way. Eating earlier in the day—as opposed to during the night—also reduces your risk of weight gain. Start this by trying to eat three-quarters of your daily meals before 2pm and add protein to your breakfast, in order to reduce the craving for extra food.

Guideline 3: Eat Consistently—and Automatically—from Day to Day

While we might like a little variation in our lives, our bodies don't. Our bodies need consistency to function, so we need to eat regularly. We can still try changing up recipes or trying new foods, but we need to put ourselves in a pattern in order to best encourage healthy eating habits.

Guideline 4: Stop Stereotyping Food

While we might associate, say, eggs with breakfast, there is no reason for this to be the case. Feel free to mix and match what you eat when. For best results, a breakfast should contain fat, protein, and whole grains. Dinners should be our smallest meal of the day, ideally something with a lot of leafy greens. To start this, begin planning your meals, but remember—you don't have to do all this at once. Following this plan will also lead to fasting for twelve hours during the night, which will provide additional benefits; however, you can extend the fasting window by a few hours if you really want to.

Recap of chapter 3

1. Eat during the day, mostly during a consistent twelve-hour window.
2. Front-load the majority of your calories for the morning and eat less at night.
3. Eat consistently from day-to-day.
4. Don't stereotype certain types of food as belonging to a certain meal (i.e. eggs for breakfast or a feast at dinner) and eat when is most *beneficial* to you.

CHAPTER 4: THE WHEN WAY: A 31-DAY PLAN

<u>SUMMARY</u>

We live in a world that likes things to happen quickly, and better eating is one of those things. Learning the Way of When and better eating doesn't take an entire century to master, but it is something that takes time. Because of this, we've created a thirty-one day plan.

The Goal: Eat Better Foods at Better Times

You should gradually shift the foods you eat, moving from less healthy processed food to whole foods. Gradually, your diet should shift to really emphasize: non-starchy vegetables (such as broccoli, onions, etc.) over starchy ones, which may spike your blood sugar; whole grains; healthy fats; proteins; and fruit, particularly berries.

Your non-starchy vegetables are numerous but typically include your leafy greens, eggplant, peppers, onions, and squash. Cooked and cooled potatoes along with green bananas are also good options—as long as you don't fry them! Healthy fats include extra-virgin olive oil, small quantities of nuts and avocado. Whole grains, of which you should have four servings daily, include buckwheat, millet, popcorn, quinoa, wild rice, and many others. Plant and sea-based proteins like fish and skinless turkey are good, also.

You will want to limit animal proteins such as red meat and egg yolks. Dairy, aside from plain, non-flavored Greek yogurt, should also mostly be avoided. Other things to consume sparingly include starchy vegetables, cheese, and alcohol. Especially reduce the amount of sugary drinks and desserts, syrups, fried foods, coconut oil, and processed foods you consume.

The Prep: What Kind of Eater Are You?

Calculate when you eat your largest meals and make slow adjustments. Look at when you eat your largest meals and try to move them earlier in the day. If you find yourself getting hungry during the transition, you may add salads or vegetables. You can also try eating pears for dessert and giving yourself a snack before dinner in order to help your body adjust. If you tend to be prone to midnight snacks, count those towards your dinner and try to work those out. Late night snacks are the worst for the body.

Recap of chapter 4

1. You do not have to become a healthy eating guru overnight; instead, keep track of your progress and slowly work towards better eating over a month-long period.
2. Work towards incorporating more leafy greens, healthy fats, and whole grains and less processed foods, unhealthy fats, starchy vegetables, and sugary desserts.
3. Eliminate those late night snacks.

CHAPTER 5: FOOD FOR THOUGHT

SUMMARY

Mindless eating is one of the things that leads to overeating. Instead, we want to focus on *mindful* eating, where we slow down and really think about what we're putting in our bodies. Slowing down and paying attention to what we're eating is the key to eating healthy. Not only does this help us eat healthy, but it also helps us enjoy food.

Make Place a Priority

We're usually very busy all the time, but when we eat, we need to focus not only on the *when* but on the *where* and *what*. We need to learn to slow down and enjoy our food, rather than grabbing something on the go all the time. If you already do this, that's great! If not, it's good to start with one meal a week, making sure that meal is away from work and distractions. We should also focus on being satisfied rather than full, which is easier to do when we slow down and really take the time to enjoy our food.

Taste and Smell

Taste and smell go hand-in-hand. Practice really savoring the food you eat, especially natural foods. Our fondness for over-processed foods has, in many ways, given many foods—such as healthy leafy greens—a reputation for being flavorless, when they are, in fact, packed with good, fresh flavors. Enjoy its flavors and the smells of it. Practice smelling and trying different foods, and don't be afraid of spices. Mix it up and try different ones. Food is meant to be experienced with multiple senses, not just thoughtlessly consumed. If you do have trouble smelling, there are small things that you can do which may help. Try drinking a lot of water or taking a ten-minute walk before meals, which will invigorate your senses.

Recap of chapter 5

1. We should focus on eating mindfully and slowing down.
2. Remember to consider the place when you eat, choosing a place that is calm and free of stressful distractions.
3. Take the time to taste and smell your food. Enjoy it.

PART 3: WHAT TO EAT WHEN

CHAPTER 6: WHEN YOU'RE STRESSED AND HANGRY

SUMMARY

It is very tempting for us to eat impulsively when we're stressed. Emotional eating is linked to biology, and while giving into temptation may temporarily help, it will harm us in the long-run. The first rule of avoiding stress eating is not to go near fast food restaurants; avoid them like the Plague.

If you're satisfied from eating during the day, you're less likely to have the urge to eat when you're stressed. However, it's also a good idea to come up with your own emergency response to situations where you might be stressed. You might keep a stash of healthy food in case of moments like these. You may also try muting your TV during advertisements or altering your commute from work, so you don't pass the tempting fast food restaurants.

Roasted chickpeas are the ideal food to eat when you're stressed. They're tasty and have numerous health benefits. However, in a pinch, butter-free popcorn will work wonders, and its flavor can be improved with sea salt, cinnamon, or other spices. It's okay to indulge in a small dessert every now and then, but desserts shouldn't be your go-to snack when you're stressed. The sugar eaten will lead to a hard and miserable crash later.

Recap of chapter 6

1. While it is tempting to eat junk when we're stressed, we should try our best not to.

2. When we're stressed, we're more susceptible to wanting fast food, so it's best to try and steer our commutes away from fast food places.

3. It doesn't hurt, though, to keep an emergency stash of healthy foods—such as roasted chickpeas or butter-free popcorn—on hand to help us when we have the impulse to eat out of stress.

CHAPTER 7: WHEN YOU'RE FEELING FATIGUED

SUMMARY

There are numerous reasons why we feel fatigued, and often, it's just not that easy to figure out why we're feeling so tired. Maybe it's stress; maybe it's sleep. Whatever the reason—or reasons— the root for much of our fatigue is food, which makes sense. Food is, after all, the source of all energy, so eating unhealthy foods can result in us feeling tired. Unfortunately, in an attempt to get energy, many of us turn to unhealthy or artificial sources, which leads to an energy crash later. This only worsens our fatigue.

Fortunately, good sleep, exercise, and stress management can all help combat fatigue. However, eating the right food can also do a lot for making us less tired. If we start our day with eating the right foods, we can cook up a recipe for a less tired, more fulfilling day.

Your Fuel Tank: Keep It Filled

Water is a key component of being healthy, and the lack of water can lead to fatigue. While eight glasses of water is the age-old recommendation, it doesn't hurt to get a half-gallon jug and drink it down each day. This saves you the trouble of having to keep up with the number of glasses you've had.

Healthy, unsaturated fats along with proteins are good ways to start the day and can help prevent fatigue as the day wears on. Coffee and tea are good for a quick burst, and they typically don't result in a crash like sugary snacks might. However, keep in mind that coffee and tea are great *if* they aren't loaded down with syrups, sugars, and artificial flavors. Complex carbohydrates are also a good choice; not only will they satisfy the craving for carbohydrates, but they will do so without resulting in a miserable crash later in the day.

Recap of chapter 7

1. Drinking the appropriate amount of water is key in helping combat fatigue.
2. We can also beat fatigue by beginning our days right and front-loading with healthy, unsaturated fats and proteins.
3. Coffee and tea might help us get through the day, and these are good choices—provided they aren't loaded up with creams, sugars, and syrups.

CHAPTER 8: WHEN YOU'RE BUMMED

<u>SUMMARY</u>

We all have moments when we're feeling down, even the happiest of us, and often, these moments lead to us craving the sweet embrace of sugary goodness. This is partly biological; our bodies want nutrients and energy to make us happy and pick us up. The trick is in finding a way to override our instinctive desire to indulge in sugar and regain the energy we've lost. However, drowning our sorrows in sugar is far from being the healthiest idea.

If you happen to be feeling down, carbohydrates are a good way to turn things around. A good thing to kick those blues away is peanut butter toast—no sugar added—although perhaps, with some berries. Peanuts, in particular, are a good choice because they include one of the building blocks of serotonin, a chemical which makes us happy.

Eating fish, vegetables, and healthy oils is a good way to help yourself in the long-term. Eating these will not only improve your mood, but some studies indicate that this diet may also reduce the risk of you developing depression. Overall, fish and omega-3 oils are the best food to eat in order to improve your mood. Another good idea for the long-term is green tea, which is not only delicious but also has proven to be very calming.

Recap of chapter 8

1. While our first instinct may be to eat a lot of sugar when we're sad, this is not a good idea.

2. Instead, healthy carbohydrates—such as peanut butter toast—are a good way to lighten our mood.

3. In the long-term, fish and green tea can't be beat for kicking away our blues.

CHAPTER 9: WHEN YOU'RE EXPERIENCING GRIEF

SUMMARY

Grieving is exhausting and emotionally draining, and the absolute last thing on anyone's mind when they've lost a loved one is what they're going to eat or make for dinner. However, there are numerous ways to look after your health when you are, understandably, experiencing very complicated and natural emotions.

The first thing to do is be willing to accept help from your friends and family. While you may impulsively want to brush off such assistance for many reasons, there's nothing wrong with accepting it, particularly during such a difficult time. Don't be afraid either to tell your friends or relatives about what foods you really like or to ask a friend to create a meal plan for you, which would let you express your desires without feeling like you're imposing.

The second thing to look at is your food. Stick with what food is familiar with you. The familiarity of foods and routine has been shown to help people cope when they are grieving. And if you need to go to the grocery store but can't muster up the energy for a full trip, stick to the express lane for quick in-and-out trips. Simply having food in your pantry can do a lot to help, and again, don't be afraid to ask for help. A friend or a loved one would probably be more than happy to go to the grocery store on your behalf. Following these steps will allow you to get good, nutritious food rather than simply eating pre-packaged junk that's easy and at hand.

Try to come up with a pattern for what you eat. Maybe you eat the same food for breakfast or lunch. While this routine might normally seem repetitive, adopting a familiar routine when you're grieving will only help you during this difficult time.

Recap of chapter 9

1. When you're grieving, accept help, and if family members offer to make you food, don't hesitate to tell them what you like.

2. If you are too emotionally exhausted to make a full trip to the grocery store, use the express lane or have a friend or loved one make the trip for you.

3. Establish a routine with what you eat; routines, while normally boring, will only help you when you're grieving.

CHAPTER 10: WHEN YOU CANNOT SLEEP

<u>SUMMARY</u>

Sleep, while crucial for our lives and health, has long been swept under a rug. While we pay a lot of attention to obesity and cigarette addiction, our lack of sleep gets relatively little attention. This is unfortunate but lack sleep, as much as the others, can be harmful for our health. The lack of sleep can even kill us.

While we sleep, our brain goes through cycles of light sleep and deep sleep. Because sleep feels like nothing is going on, we tend to ignore it. However, this is not the case. While we're sleeping, our bodies are hard at work repairing and fixing themselves. During the day, our bodies work hard and get very tired, and we need sleep to help us repair ourselves from working all day. When we don't get enough sleep, our body doesn't get repaired properly, and it can increase our health risks. One of the most dangerous risks of not getting enough sleep is high inflammatory response, which puts us at an increased risk of developing heart disease, diabetes, and arthritis.

When we don't get enough sleep, we're also tired, and because our bodies want energy, we want to eat sugar. Obviously, this is easier said than done, but we do need to consider sleep when we're making lifestyle changes. And one of the ways we can do this is through food. There is no specific sleep-inducing food, but we can arrange our eating schedule to help us sleep better.

Key Players

Magnesium and tryptophan are two crucial nutrients for encouraging better sleeping habits. These nutrients help us get better sleep quality and can be found in foods such as egg whites, soybeans, chicken, and pumpkin seeds.

Avoid the midnight snacks and instead eat a fiber-rich dessert before you go to bed. A pear is a good option because the fiber will help you feel full for longer.

Recap of chapter 10

1. Sleep is crucial for being healthy because our bodies repair themselves when we're sleeping.
2. Eating foods that contain magnesium and tryptophan can help encourage better quality sleep.
3. Eating fiber-rich desserts is a good way of curbing the desire for less healthy midnight snacks.

CHAPTER 11: WHEN YOU GET A LOT OF HEADACHES

SUMMARY

Unfortunately, there are some headaches which cannot be beaten into submission with Ibuprofen and sleep. Even worse, there is no singular solution for them. Headaches have many causes, including hormones, changes in diet, medications, environmental factors, toxins, or stress. And some of us may get headaches throughout our lives.

Headaches also have different causes. Usually, they occur because of certain changes to our cranial nerves. However, headaches can also come from the muscles around our heads.

Because the causes and treatments of headaches are so numerous and different, there is no guarantee that any one thing will work. Food can also often be a trigger for headaches, so knowing what you eat and how it affects your body can help. It's important to begin a food and headache journal if you have frequent headaches. You may begin to notice patterns for which foods may be triggering your headaches. Keep in mind that these headaches can occur within a twelve-hour window of eating the triggering food. If you have persistent headaches, you should learn to adjust your diet in order to lessen the chances of having headaches.

Key Players

When trying to reduce headaches, leafy greens are a godsend. Egg whites are also a good food to eat that can help prevent or lessen headaches. And because a common cause of frequent headaches is a lack of magnesium, eating foods with magnesium—such as seeds and nuts—are a good idea. It may also be a good idea to cut alcohol, specifically red wines, from your diet. Not only does alcohol potentially cause dehydration, but tannins, a substance found in red wines, can also be triggers for headaches.

Try substituting potentially triggering foods. Red meat can be replaced with fish, artificial sweeteners in coffee can be replaced with a pinch of cinnamon, chocolate can be replaced with walnuts and berries, and soy sauce can be switched out with other spices.

Recap of chapter 11

1. Headaches have many causes and many cures and are not a one-size-fits-all.

2. Keeping track of foods that may trigger headaches and switching them out with other foods may lessen the number of headaches you have.

3. Headaches are also often the result of a lack of magnesium, so eating magnesium-rich foods may also help lessen them.

CHAPTER 12: WHEN YOU'RE SICK

SUMMARY

We all get sick sometimes. Whether it's the cold or just a few crappy days, we all have situations where we're just feeling a little down. Some of us get sicker than others, and while no food can provide a magical cure for the cold or the flu, food can still play a crucial role in how we keep ourselves healthy and lessen our chances of getting sick.

While there is disagreement over how much vitamin C and zinc help us—say—get over the common cold, they will still help us in the long run. There is a lot of debate about how food impacts us when we're ill, but the easy answer is that we should listen to our bodies. If we can eat, we should because our bodies need nutrients; however, if we're feeling sick and don't want to eat, we shouldn't force ourselves to.

What to Eat

While it's a cliché, studies have proven that chicken soup really does help when it comes to helping us feel better when we're sick. Other foods that help us are garlic, which can boost our immune systems and help us keep from getting colds. Ginger has also shown to help us, and mushrooms have been proven to help prevent infection. You may also eat zinc-rich foods, but make sure not to overdo it. Too much zinc can be toxic.

When you're sick to your stomach, you can substitute many foods in order to make yourself feel better. Substitute orange juice, which can have a lot of sugar, for an orange. When you're sick and your immune system is compromised, it's a good idea to replace sushi with salmon or trout. Chia seeds may be great, but when you're sick and potentially dehydrated, it's best to replace them with waterlogged oatmeal or something similar.

Recap of chapter 12

1. It's important to eat good food, with nutrients such a vitamin C, to help us prevent getting sick.
2. When we are sick, chicken soup, garlic, ginger, and mushrooms can help us get well quickly.
3. When we're sick, we also want to eat wisely in order to compensate for our compromised immune systems by replacing certain foods—orange juice for oranges, sushi for cooked salmon or trout, and chia seeds with waterlogged oatmeal.

CHAPTER 13: WHEN YOU'RE IN PAIN

SUMMARY

There are many different kinds of pain. There is, of course, emotional pain and a scale of physical pain. There is also chronic pain, which impacts numerous Americans.

Emotional pain is easy to understand. Something occurs and causes you pain for a while, but eventually, this pain goes away. Physical pain is a little trickier because it can have any number of reasons for happening, and sometimes, it's hard to stop. Chronic pain might also be hard to understand, and if you are having chronic pain, it's crucial to do physical therapy (PT) to help. There are also numerous foods that can help make chronic pain more manageable.

Notably, it is important to know that pain is not inherently bad. Pain is our brain telling us that something is wrong or needs to be fixed. While eating good foods won't miraculously heal everything, they will help your body in the long-term, so it's easier to manage pain.

MVP

Research indicates that people who follow a Mediterranean based diet experience less problems with inflammation, including joint problems. Thus, extra virgin olive oil and walnuts are very good for encouraging preventative care. Olive oil also includes healthy omega-3 oils, which are crucial for staying healthy, so it's a great choice for cooking food in. When fighting inflammation, spicy foods are also a good choice. Ginger, in particular, has proven to be successful. Replacing sugary foods and carbs are also a good way to help your body feel better.

Recap of chapter 13

1. If you are in chronic pain, you should have physical therapy to help you better manage it.
2. Pain is not inherently bad; it tells us when we need to make changes.
3. To lessen inflammation and pain, we should eat Mediterranean based diets including olive oil and walnuts.
4. Spicy foods and ginger are also good for preventing inflammation.
5. In order to manage pain, we should cut out sugary foods and carbs, which will help our body feel better in the long-term.

CHAPTER 14: WHEN YOU HAVE DIGESTIVE PROBLEMS

SUMMARY

Digestion is a very complicated process but crucial because it helps process and break down our food. Food moves from esophagus to stomach, breaking down acids and enzymes. It then moves to the intestines, where it is broken down, absorbed into the bloodstream, and transferred through the rest of the body. Sometimes, this does not go as planned. Our stomachs rumble and cramp, and we experience digestive problems.

There are many reasons for digestive problems, some relating to the microbiome, our gut bacteria. Sometimes, this can become unbalanced because of the foods we eat or because of various intolerances—such as those to lactose or gluten. It is, therefore, important to pin down the causes of these problems.

Diarrhea/Vomiting

Diarrhea and vomiting are two common digestive problems, and if you're experiencing one of these, you likely won't want to eat much. The exception is the BRAT diet—bananas, rice, apples, and toast. These are gentle on your stomach and can help ease diarrhea and vomiting.

A lot of diarrhea can also cause dehydration, which can be combatted by making an oral rehydration solution (ORS) made of six teaspoons sugar, ½ teaspoon of salt, and a liter of water. This is a rare time where it's okay to have sugar because it replaces electrolytes.

Constipation

When you're constipated, the CRAP diet—cranberries, raisins, apricots, and prunes—are very effective in helping you get past constipation. Because constipation also creates dehydration, you should also drink water when you're constipated.

Reflux

When you have reflux or heartburn, it's best to look at making changes to what you're eating. Look at avoiding foods that are spicy as well as caffeine and alcohol. Cutting back on chocolate and citric foods may also help. However, you can also try changing your behaviors after you eat. For example, not going straight to bed after eating might alleviate reflux.

Bloating

Bloating and its causes vary, but one way to reduce bloating is to eat more slowly, which will cut down on the amount of air you consume while you eat. Eating slow-digesting carbohydrates, such as fiber and a lot of vegetables, can also help reduce bloating.

Recap of chapter 14

1. There are many reasons we might have digestive problems.
2. When you have diarrhea and vomiting, it's important to stay hydrated and eat the BRAT (bananas, rice, apples, and toast) diet.

3. Constipation can be lessened by eating the CRAP (cranberries, raisins, apricots, and prunes) diet.
4. Reflux can be managed by altering the foods you eat, specifically by cutting out spicy food along with caffeine and alcohol.
5. Bloating can be lessened by eating more slowly and opting for slow-digesting carbohydrates.

CHAPTER 15: WHEN YOU'RE BEING TESTED

SUMMARY

Whether it's a test for college, a certification exam, or a request to do something for our boss last-minute, we're tested all the time. To help us perform at our peak mental performance, we should eat brain-friendly foods.

Key Players

Coffee and green tea work wonders when we need something to help us focus in a pinch. This is why caffeine has become so popular for starting the morning. Caffeine makes more neurons fire, which is good. Ideally, you want one or two cups of coffee or tea at approximately thirty minutes before the test.

Another good idea is to eat a meal with whole grains, slow-digesting carbohydrates that will provide you with the pinch of energy you need to keep going. A whole wheat English muffin with sugar-free peanut butter makes an ideal snack for situations like these.

Although it's tempting to reach for something in the vending machine down the hall, try to resist. These snacks may initially feel good, but once they're sugary goodness fades, you'll crash, which is definitely not what you want.

Recap of chapter 15

1. Tea and coffee are ideal drinks for when you need to focus on any important mental task.

2. Slow digesting carbohydrates are also good for keeping focused.

3. Resist anything you find in the vending machine; it might help you in the short-term, but the sudden burst of energy will quickly crash.

CHAPTER 16: WHEN YOU HAVE A JOB INTERVIEW

SUMMARY

When you have a job interview, you want to make sure you've done as much as you can to succeed. You've picked out the right clothes and practiced answering common questions, but you can also pick foods to help you stay sharp and energetic for your important interview.

A good way to begin your morning is with whole grains, perhaps, with some added flax. This provides alpha-linolenic, which improves mental performance. Flax also contains crucial B vitamins, which increase energy and improve focus. Coffee in small amounts is also a good idea, but don't drink so much you're jumping off the walls.

For best results, eat ninety minutes before your interview if you can. This will give your food time to partially digest, which will mean you aren't attending your interview with a bloated or empty stomach. This window of time also allows you plenty of energy during your interview. It's a good idea to make a meal that includes all three of your macronutrients—perhaps, a chicken sandwich on whole wheat with a slice of avocado. Alternatively, you might also opt for nuts and fruit. Just before your interview, go for a cup or two of coffee to improve your focus.

For the interview itself, all you need is a bottle of water. This will not only prevent your throat from drying out, but it will help you maintain your focus throughout. A bag of nuts also is a good idea if you're doing multiple meetings back-to-back and may not have time to sit down for an entire meal.

Recap of chapter 16

1. The morning of an important interview, it's a good idea to begin with whole grains, perhaps, with added flax.
2. Eat a meal ninety minutes before your interview, preferably one that includes the three macronutrients.
3. A cup or two of coffee might be helpful for improving alertness during interviews.
4. Take a bottle of water with you to your interview, to prevent your throat from drying out but also to help increase your alertness.

CHAPTER 17: WHEN YOU HAVE TO MAKE A BIG DECISION

SUMMARY

Everyone has to make decisions, and obviously food is not the sole deciding factor in most of our decisions. However, because food affects many things—including our moods, emotions, and health—it is important to take into consideration. It is crucial to look at what factors can influence us when we make decisions, and then, we should look at how food can impact those factors.

Sleep is the foremost important of these factors. Getting enough sleep can help us make decisions with a clear and rested mind, which makes it easier for us to weigh our decisions. We can eat the When Way in order to make our sleep better.

Because we want to make clear decisions, we should avoid making decisions while drinking alcohol or on an empty stomach. One way of helping us make these clear decisions is by eating brain-healthy foods, such as those containing omega-3 oils. We can also help ourselves a lot by consuming small amounts of caffeine by drinking tea or coffee.

Recap of chapter 17

1. Many factors can influence us when we make decisions.
2. To make good decisions, we should be sure we're getting enough sleep, which is more likely if we're eating the When Way.

3. Eating foods rich in omega-3 oils as well as drinking reasonable amounts of coffee and tea can help us think clearly and make better decisions.

CHAPTER 18: WHEN YOU'RE ON THE GO

SUMMARY

The key to eating healthy is control, but having control isn't always easy. We live very busy lives and don't always have time to sit down and eat a carefully-constructed meal. Sometimes, we have to eat on the go, and the gas station is the only option. If this happens, we should strategize and look for the healthiest options available.

Bags of nuts, preferably unsalted and without honey and sugar, are a good option and available at most gas stations. These provide protein and energy. Water is also the best choice for hydration, but you can also grab a cup of coffee or water. Just skip the sugar and milk. Fruit packs—not of the gummy variety, but of sliced fruit—are also a good option of an on-the-go snack. A cup of Greek yogurt is also a good choice, if you can find it. Finally, hummus is a great snack, filled with healthy fat and protein.

Just be careful. A lot of so-called "healthy" items like granola bars and trail mix are loaded up with extra sugars. The same is true of beef jerky. And if you can't avoid the siren's call of the fountain drink machine, grab some crushed ice and a couple of bottles of sparkling water.

Recap of chapter 18

1. If you have to eat on the go, eat wisely.
2. Eat nuts, packs of sliced fruit, Greek yogurt, and hummus; drink water, coffee, or tea if you're in a pinch.
3. Be careful with healthy-sounding foods like granola bars and trail mix; these can have a lot of hidden sugar.

CHAPTER 19: WHEN YOU HAVE AN EVENT

SUMMARY

No matter where you work, this work will probably overlap with your eating schedule at some point. It might be in the employee breakroom, a vending machine, or an invitation to go out for lunch or for an after-work dinner. Unfortunately, planning and preparing your own meals, while working to be healthy, is quite different from trying to be healthy while being surrounded by unhealthy food that everyone else is eating. Mind you; there's nothing wrong with a little, occasional indulgence, but this doesn't need to be a frequent affair.

When navigating these social functions, there are many measures you can take beforehand to minimize the desire to eat unhealthy foods. The first is to prepare beforehand by eating a couple of apples, which will provide you with nutrients and fiber, thereby lessening the temptation to overeat unhealthy food.

Water and coffee are also good. Staying hydrated will help fight the temptation for alcoholic drinks, and coffee will provide something to drink and give your hands something to do, making it easier to avoid the snacks being passed around.

If you're at a buffet, make sure to look over everything before you take something. While limitless food may make you want to grab everything, this is not the best thing to do. Also, keep in mind that you're at a work function, which might mean you're more likely to eat without thinking.

While you may not always succeed eating healthy at every

work function, try to promise yourself to eat some leafy greens and lean protein. Then, you can sprinkle in a few less healthy foods.

Recap of chapter 19

1. When attending a work function that involves food, eat a couple of apples beforehand, to minimize the desire to eat everything and anything.
2. Drink water and/or coffee, both for hydration and to keep your hands busy, cutting back on mindless eating.
3. If you're attending a work function with a buffet, look over everything before choosing something to eat; this will help you keep from overeating everything.

CHAPTER 20: WHEN YOU'RE ON VACATION

SUMMARY

When we're on vacation, we need time to relax and enjoy a break, and having a couple indulgent days of eating isn't going to be the end of the world. However, doing so for an attended amount of time might make it hard for you to keep to following the When Way and eating healthy. The best way to stay on track is to plan beforehand. Eat healthy on the go and make one of your first stops the local grocery store. You can stock up on healthy snacks and even cook a few healthy meals.

Other ways to keep eating healthy on vacation include splitting meals, which will save both calories and money, particularly if you're traveling with a family. You can also ask restaurants to make small changes in order to make your food healthier. You, can, for example, substitute fries for fresh vegetables.

You can also stay on track by strategizing when you're going to eat, arranging it around the other events during your vacation. You can also pay attention to the sides you might eat, making sure that those healthy-sounding vegetables aren't secretly drenched in butter. As always, drinking a lot of water and staying hydrated is important, too. Also, keep in mind that you can certainly try local foods, but you don't have to clear your entire plate.

Recap of chapter 20

1. It's okay to indulge a little on vacation, but don't go overboard.
2. Strategies such as splitting meals, substituting for healthier sides, arranging your eating into your schedule, paying attention to sides, and staying hydrated can help you stay on track while on vacation.
3. Remember that you don't have to clear your plate at every single meal; you can try new things without over-indulging.

CHAPTER 21: WHEN IT'S THE HOLIDAY SEASON

SUMMARY

Most holidays are associated with unhealthy food. Whether it's the candy for Valentine's Day or Halloween, the cakes at birthday parties, or the New Year's champagne, holidays are frequently synonymous with sugar. Obviously, you don't have to cut out all sugar ever, but it's crucial to practice moderation in order to maintain healthy eating habits during the holidays. Eating a high-fiber snack such as an apple before going to a holiday party can help ward away cravings.

MVP

Water is crucial during the holidays. Not only can it help you stay hydrated, thereby curbing the desire to binge-eat a hundred mini Snicker bars. Keeping a glass of water in hand, particularly at a holiday party which might involve shaking a lot of hands, leaves no hands left to grab a quick snack with.

Also, scope out the veggie tray. Not only does these leafy green vegetables provide much needed nutrients, they also have fiber, which will help curb your appetite and lessen the temptation to mindlessly eat sweets.

Cut from the Team

While a little poor eating around the holidays is acceptable, we do want to try and cut out sweets that aren't made with whole grains. You also want to try and avoid saturated fat and partially hydrogenated oils, both often found in sweets.

To be healthier, let go of the self-basting turkeys and instead baste your turkey with a broth, either made or a pre-made, low sodium option. Also, cook the stuffing outside of the turkey in order to prevent it from soaking up fat. It's also a good idea to avoid using thickeners like flour and cornstarch in your gravy.

Recap of chapter 21

1. During the holidays, it's okay to indulge a little bit, but don't go overboard.
2. Drinking water during holiday parties is a good way to keep yourself from overeating or from drinking to many alcohol beverages.
3. If you are going to indulge a bit, try to avoid desserts including saturated fat and partially hydrogenated oils.
4. Skip the self-basting turkeys and opt for basting yourself with homemade or pre-made, low sodium broth.

CHAPTER 22: WHEN YOU'RE AT THE STADIUM

SUMMARY

When you go to the stadium or to the ballpark, there are often a myriad of unhealthy, ballpark snacks. Rather than going for the first deep-fried creation you see, try bringing your own healthy snack, if you're allowed to. If you can't bring your own food in, try eating a healthy meal or snack before you go. Also, drink lots of water; this will help lessen your cravings to eat unhealthy food at the stadium. You may also look for healthier snacks when you're at the stadium.

MVPs

When you're at the stadium, peanuts are often by far the best choice. These will also keep you fuller for longer, and if they're peanuts that require shelling, they will also help slow down your eating, preventing you from eating as much.

At some stadiums, you may find turkey sausage or grilled chicken sandwiches, which are a great substitute for burger and hot dogs, particularly if you eat these two without the bun.

You want to avoid wings, cheesesteaks, nachos, soda, and many other stadium foods. Obviously, the occasional one won't be the end of the world, but too many can really wreck with your attempts to eat the When Way.

Recap of chapter 22

1. Instead of going for the first fried food you find, bring healthy snacks if you can.

2. If you do eat at the stadium, peanuts are the best option by far, but turkey sausage and grilled chicken sandwiches sans bun are also good options.

3. Keep the usual, stereotypical stadium foods—such as nachos, sodas, etc.—to a minimum.

CHAPTER 23: WHEN YOU'RE ON A FIRST DATE

SUMMARY

Today, a first date may not be the actual first time you see your date. You've probably texted or messaged before, but that doesn't mean the first date is any less special. You want the date to go well. Obviously, there's no need to talk about how you should behave on a date. We all know not to spend the date on our cell phones or to talk so much our date can't get a word in edgewise. Often, though, first dates happen over a meal.

So what do you eat? A good first date would include a salad, sans dressing—unless it's oil and vinegar. If you're eating marinara, you also want it on the side, so as to minimize the temptation to eat it. Ordering dark chocolate, which has health benefits, is a good choice, and as an added bonus, it helps reduce anxiety.

Unfortunately, none of the popular aphrodisiacs—oysters, asparagus, chocolate, and avocados—actually do anything to increase your libido, but they're still healthy options for eating. If you're looking for pre-date meals, it's best to go with foods that slowly increase energy levels, such as walnuts, slices of turkey, and avocado toast.

Obviously, this might all be a little much for the first date, but if more dates happen, it's important to note your new partner's eating habits and how they match against yours.

Recap of chapter 23

1. A good first date should include salad, although make sure to avoid the unhealthy dressings.
2. If you're ordering food with marinara, have it on the side.
3. Dark chocolate is a good food for reducing anxiety.
4. So-called aphrodisiacs—oysters, dark chocolate, and avocados—have no basis in science, but they're still healthy foods to consider.
5. For meals before the date, look at foods which release energy slowly.

CHAPTER 24: WHEN YOU EXERCISE

SUMMARY

Exercise, of course, has numerous health benefits and is key to living a healthy lifestyle. Along with food, exercise is one of the cornerstones to living a healthy, fruitful lifestyle. We're going to assume that if you're eating the When Way, you're probably also doing some sort of exercise regularly. Maybe it's walking or resistance training. Maybe it's something more grueling. Exercise has a wide range of forms and benefits, which makes it difficult to generalize your nutritional needs.

Don't Overcompensate

When you exercise regularly, it's tempting to eat to much. Because we burn so many calories when we exercise, it's tempting to fall into a cycle of thinking we can eat extra because we've put in the work to exercise; however, our bodies don't quite work that way. While it's true that we burn calories when we exercise, those calories are not the whole of what we're going to consume that day. We still need to make good choices about what we're eating and how much.

Eating After Generally Trumps Eating Before

In most cases, it's best to eat after a workout rather than before one. Our bodies use glucose primarily for energy, but when we eat, our bodies store some energy for later, long-term use. This is where fat comes in. If we exercise, then, after a period of not eating—such as in the morning after sleeping—it's easier for us to get to that fat and start burning it right away.

Additionally, eating after rather than before will encourage your muscles to repair damage they might have incurred during your exercise.

Experiment!

All athletes have diets that they specifically tailor to themselves, and we should be no exception. It's a good idea to experiment with what you eat because exercise has so many different variables and factors to consider.

Grilled skinless chicken is probably the best, generalized choice for your work-out diet. It's definitely a food you want if you exercise regularly. This lean protein helps you rebuild muscle, and it contains selenium, an element which helps your muscles function properly.

Canned black beans and sweet potatoes are also excellent additions to your diet. This helps both cholesterol levels and helps you feel fuller after exercise if it leaves you hungry. It's also, of course, a good source of vitamins and minerals. You also want to cut out the daily treat. While an occasional reward is fine, this isn't a free pass to load up on sugary confectionaries and unhealthy carbs.

Recap of chapter 24

1. Exercise if crucial for living a healthy lifestyle.

2. For best results, you usually want to eat before rather than after a workout.

3. Experiment with your diet for best results.

4. Grilled chicken, black beans, and sweet potatoes are excellent foods for keeping your muscles healthy after exercise.

5. Try to resist the sweet siren's call of eating too many sugary rewards for exercising.

CHAPTER 25: WHEN YOU'RE TRYING TO GET PREGNANT (OR ALREADY ARE)

SUMMARY

While we usually think of pregnancy as the result of what happens between two people in the bedroom, numerous factors can influence fertility, and food is one of those factors. The most obvious one is that the healthier you are, the better your chances of carrying a healthy baby to term. This means maintaining a healthy weight, often affected by the food you eat, and by eating extra nutrients once you are pregnant, to the benefit of both your baby and yourself.

When You're Trying to Get Pregnant

Obviously, fertility is complicated and depends on many factors, including genetics, and there is no magical food that can suddenly make you have a baby. If you're under thirty-five and have been trying unsuccessfully to get pregnant for over a year, it's a good idea to talk with a specialist to address any underlying issues. There are many different issues that can cause infertility in women. These might be physical, chemical, or infections. They might also have to do with the way the egg is being fertilized. Stress can also contribute to infertility, which is a good reason to eat healthily; eating the right foods can help you feel less stressed. It's also a good idea to take prenatal supplements.

When You Are Pregnant

While it's a commonly heard cliché for pregnant women to be "eating for two," this isn't meant to be interpreted literally. You need a little more food than usual but definitely not twice the normal amount. You also want to eat a lot of healthy foods and really minimize unhealthy ones. You also want to be wary of mercury high foods, such as tuna, which can be harmful to the baby you're trying to conceive.

MVPs

Grilled salmon salad comes highly recommended. Not only is salmon full of omega-3, healthy fat oils that your baby needs, but it's also a fish with the lowest risk of carrying mercury. The omega-3 oils will also help your hormones, while the leafy greens in the salad will help aid in fetal development.

You also want to increase the amount of dairy that you're taking in. This will help your bones stay strong, but research indicates it may also help women who have difficulty ovulating. Just be careful about what dairy you're drinking. Because non-fat dairy might increase the risk of infertility, you need to watch the amount of fat you're drinking. Icelandic and Greek yogurt, fortunately, are both low-fat and good sources of dairy.

Avoid fish that carries a high risk of mercury. This includes tuna, obviously, but also swordfish, shark, and other saltwater fish.

Recap of chapter 25

1. While fertility depends on many factors, many of the factors that might cause infertility, like stress, can be combated with proper, healthy eating.

2. When pregnant, grilled salmon salad is a perfect source of nutrients for you and your growing child.

3. When pregnant, avoid high-mercury fish like tuna.

4. Increase your dairy intake, but keep an eye on the amount of fat you're consuming; consider opting for Greek or Icelandic yogurt as good dairy alternatives.

CHAPTER 26: WHEN YOU'RE NURSING

SUMMARY

Obviously, mothers do a lot for their children, and one of the most crucial of these things, from day one, is nursing. When you're a nursing mother, what you eat is the same thing that your baby eats. Thus, your choices of foods are crucial because they are actively affecting another human being on a deep, biological level. Of course, there are other options besides breastfeeding. Mothers may choose formula or a combination of the two, which can be used to great effect.

Breast milk, firstly, contains the three macronutrients—fat, protein, and carbohydrates—which are crucial for developing your baby's brain and systems as well as for giving your baby energy. Additionally, breast milk is full of vitamins and minerals that are needed to build an effective immune system for your child. Thus, moms who are breast feeding need a healthy balanced diet containing a lot of fruits, vegetables, protein, and healthy carbs and fats. And you do burn calories while nursing, but that doesn't mean you have an excuse to engorge yourself with massive amounts of food. A little extra calories won't hurt, but you need to look at getting back to your weight pre-pregnancy and in keeping your choices healthy.

MVPs

Salmon and trout—or, for vegetarians—DHA pills are the absolute best thing to eat when you're breastfeeding because DHA helps spur brain development. If you eat more DHA, your baby will also be eating more DHA through your breast milk.

Zinc is also crucial. The best sources of zinc are oysters and other mussels, but you do not want to eat these uncooked while breastfeeding. They might have harmful bacteria or potentially viruses. Instead, focus on foods that contain legumes, such as garbanzo beans.

You want to cut foods that are uncooked or that might contain harmful things, such as bacteria or mercury. To be on the safe side, you may also want to be careful with citrus fruits, as these can sometimes cause gastrointestinal distress in babies. The safest choice, again, is salmon or trout, both of which have high amounts of healthy omega-3 oils in them.

Recap of chapter 26

1. When breastfeeding, it's important to remember that your baby is consuming that same foods that you are.
2. Breast milk contains both the three macronutrients as well as much-needed vitamins to your baby, but it is not the only option; formula and a combination of formula and breastmilk also provide needed nutrients to your baby.
3. Salmon or ocean trout are good foods to eat, as they contain healthy omega-3 oils.
4. Zinc is also important when breastfeeding.
5. When breastfeeding, it's important to avoid foods that are uncooked or high at risk for containing mercury, such as tuna.

CHAPTER 27: WHEN YOU HAVE PMS OR PERIOD PAIN

SUMMARY

The world operates in cycles, and one of those is the menstrual cycle, something which can result in many irritating and painful symptoms, depending on the woman experiencing it. It might be headaches, mood swings, cramps, bloating, and more. We know why these happen. Cramps, for example, can occur from muscles contracting and cutting off the oxygen going to the uterus. Abnormal amounts of cramping can also be a symptom of endometriosis, and unfortunately, no diet is going to fix this.

In an attempt to stop the pain of periods, women might try any number of remedies ranging from hot baths to medication. Obviously, if your periods are severe, you need to consult a professional, but if you experience only moderate symptoms, the food you eat is worth looking into.

MVPs

Celery and hummus is your best friend. Because it's filled with water and low in calories, celery can help lessen bloating, while hummus—with its combination of protein and healthy fat—can keep cramps away. Just make sure you wash that celery down with lots of water, as hydration is one of many preventative measures you can take to deal with the symptoms of your cycle.

A stash of dark chocolate doesn't hurt either, as research indicates it may help manage stress hormones. It can also curb food cravings, which may be much worse during your period. Don't overindulge, but a little bit of chocolate can work wonders.

Two things you don't want to take in during your period are alcohol and caffeine, as these can worsen symptoms. It's a good idea to try cutting these out of your diet during your period to see if anything changes, and if not, it's not a bad idea to look at eliminating other foods, particularly those that are salt and sugar-heavy.

Recap of chapter 27

1. 1.When on your period, hydration is key to preventing bloating.
2. Dark chocolate can help you manage stress and curb cravings for other, less healthy foods during your period.
3. If you have a rough time during your period, try cutting out caffeine and alcohol, as these can often worsen symptoms.

CHAPTER 28: WHEN YOU HAVE HOT FLASHES

SUMMARY

Hormones can be responsible for a lot of our bodies' ailments, and one of those is hot flashes, which occur due to a change in estrogen levels. As we age, our estrogen spikes and falls, which impacts our body's ability to keep a steady blood flow. This change alters our blood vessels, and this, combined with estrogen's role in regulating our body temperature, results in our body temperature skyrocketing. Fortunately, when we eat the When Way, we can help prevent this blood flow from fluctuating so wildly. And of course, food cannot fix everything, so if your hot flashes are causing you great discomfort, it's advised to speak to a medical professional.

MVPs

Soybeans are a great option for controlling hot flashes, and they're backed by science. It's a good idea, then, to include a lot of them in your diet. The traditional Mediterranean diet also might help as a long-term solution for some women. In fact, one study of women who ate meals of vegetables, whole grain noodles, and red wine, showed a significant reduction in the hot flashes they experienced.

You can also help lessen hot flashes by cutting caffeine out of your diet. This doesn't mean that you have to swear off all coffee; you can still have decaf and even moderate amounts of green tea.

Recap of chapter 28

1. Hot flashes are caused by our changing levels of estrogen as we get older.
2. Eating soybeans and a Mediterranean diet can help lessen the amount of hot flashes you experience.
3. Cutting out caffeine can also lessen the number of hot flashes you have.

CHAPTER 29: WHEN YOU NEED A TESTOSTERONE BOOST

SUMMARY

While testosterone is most commonly thought of as being the hormone that controls men's muscles and libido, this is not all testosterone is responsible for. In fact, women's libido is also tied to testosterone. There are a ton of supplements for improving testosterone levels, but testosterone can also be increased by weight training and by eating the right foods.

While we may associate certain symptoms with a lack of testosterone as we age, there can—in fact—be many reasons for these. Your first step shouldn't necessarily be to reach for supplements but to get to the root of your problems. The When Way emphasizes foods that may help if your testosterone levels need a boost.

A substance called resveratrol, found in red wine, is widely believed to increase levels of testosterone. While this substance is also in supplements, more is absorbed by eating it. Some studies suggest pomegranates, so fruit salad including pomegranates, grapes, and watermelon are highly recommended if you're trying to improve testosterone levels.

Cabbage with pumpkin seeds are also a good choice. Studies indicate that cabbage lowers estrogen levels, thereby lowering the risk of prostate cancer. Seeds, meanwhile, contain zinc, a lack of which is associated with lower levels of testosterone. Salmon, also, is a good food; its high levels of vitamin D may also help in increasing testosterone levels.

Recap of chapter 29

1. Testosterone is a varied hormone with many functions.
2. While many testosterone supplements exist, these are not necessarily the best choice for a long-term increase in your testosterone levels.
3. Eating fruit salads (of pomegranates, grapes, and watermelon), cabbage sprinkled with pumpkin seeds, and salmon are good foods to eat if your goal is to improve testosterone levels.

CHAPTER 30: WHEN YOU WANT TO IMPROVE FERTILITY

SUMMARY

Obviously, there are many factors that may impact fertility, enough to fill a book all on their own. For this chapter, we're only looking at sperm health. If men ejaculate, they are most likely to be fertile. Quantity is crucial, however, and studies indicate the sperm numbers appear to be going down over the years. While experts can't say for sure why this has happened, we think it's because of food choice, changes in environment, and stress.

Because sperm count is so crucial in male fertility, it's something many of us are deeply concerned about. We also need sperm that can move in order to fertilize an egg. Food comes into play in a couple of ways. Namely, research shows that sleep apnea and weight gain can be detrimental to sperm counts. Thus, better eating may reduce weight and improve fertility. That's not to say that diet works as a miracle fertility cure, but to really increase fertility, it doesn't hurt to make healthy food choices.

MVPs

Walnuts and fish are your best bets for this, as they contain ALA and omega-3 fatty acids, both of which are proven to improve the quality and quantity of sperm. It is important when eating fish—and lots of it—to seek out low-mercury varieties such as ocean trout and salmon. And walnuts, specifically, should be eaten because they're proven to decrease risks of sperm being damaged.

There are, of course, numerous other nutrients that have proven to have a positive effect on sperm. Tomatoes are a very good food option because they contain lycopene, which boosts sperm motility. Tomato sauce is even better because lycopene is more easily absorbed from a source that's been cooked.

You want to cut saturated fat, which means you want to scale back your red meat and dairy products. Research indicates that this variety of fat bears an association with lower semen quality.

Recap of chapter 30

1. There are many factors that may increase or decrease fertility, but one that can be helped through proper diet is sperm quality.
2. Walnuts and fish, and lots of them, are the best choices for improving sperm quality and quantity.
3. Tomatoes are also important, as they appear to boost sperm quality.
4. Skip out on the red meat and dairy, which lower semen quality.

CHAPTER 31: WHEN YOU NEED TO SHRINK YOUR PROSTATE

SUMMARY

An enlarged prostate can be a serious problem, potentially indicative of cancer. However, a large prostate may also be noncancerous; this latter case impacts about 10% of men but can cause considerable discomfort. This can cause trouble urinating and ejaculating. If you experience irregularities with your penis, you need to consult a professional to be sure that you don't have prostate cancer.

Some medications can help lessen the size of the prostate and alleviate the symptoms. There are also surgical solutions. However, you can help, too, by eating the When Way. Having at least four servings of vegetables a day and exercising regularly can be a big help to your prostate.

MVPs

Zinc is crucial for prostate health. However, zinc is best absorbed from your food rather than from supplements, so while it's tempting to reach for those, opt instead for spinach, which is full of this crucial vitamin.

Nuts, seeds, legumes, and beans can also have a positive effect on your prostate. In particular kidney beans, lima beans, chickpeas, peanuts, and pumpkin seeds are all excellent choices. Tomatoes, too, are a good idea.

You want to keep reducing saturated fats, particularly the ones you find in red meat. Also, look at cutting back caffeine, as it can worsen symptoms of an enlarged prostate.

Recap of chapter 31

1. If you notice problems with urinating or with your penis functioning properly, it is a good idea to talk to a medical professional.
2. Zinc is crucial for a healthy prostate, and eating spinach is a good way of getting it.
3. Nuts, seeds, and beans are good for encouraging prostate health.
4. If you do have an enlarged prostate, cut out caffeine, which can worsen the symptoms of it.

CHAPTER 32: WHEN YOU HAVE A FAMILY HISTORY OF CANCER

SUMMARY

Cancer is a hot-button issue in the medical field, and that's because it's scary. It is a very complex disease dependent on several factors, so obviously, there is no cure-all food that will magically obliterate or heal cancer. However, you can choose foods that will minimize your risk of developing cancer. Even a few changes—like exercise, eating the When Way, not smoking or drinking heavily—can drastically reduce your risk for getting cancer. The risk of death from these cancers can also be greatly reduced with proper diet and exercise.

Your immune system acts to stop diseases and viruses. You're probably at least passingly familiar with it. Sometimes, your immune system can kill cancer cells, but not always. Because cancer cells form from normal cells, sometimes, they can hide and spread. To keep your immune system in tip-top shape, though, you want to have high levels of vitamin D, known most for helping you have strong bones but also crucial in a strong immune system.

Free radicals, or oxygen reacting with certain molecules, can also cause cancer to develop. The best way to combat free radicals is with antioxidants, found particularly in fruits and vegetables. Blueberries, blackberries, raspberries, and pomegranates are the winning fruits when it comes to these.

Other good things to improve your immune system include: apples, citrus fruits, cooked tomatoes, garlic, cruciferous vegetables (like cauliflower and broccoli), and mushrooms. Coffee and tea may also lessen the risk of cancer. Cutting out red meat is also a good way to reduce the risk of cancer.

Recap of chapter 32

1. Even small changes like exercise and eating the When Way can help minimize your risk of cancer.
2. A good immune system, built by taking in vitamin D, is also crucial in lessening the risk of cancer.
3. Eating antioxidants, found often in berries, is a good way to lessen the risk of free radicals, another way cancer forms.
4. Coffee and tea may also help prevent cancer.
5. Cut out red meat to lessen the risk of cancer.

CHAPTER 33: WHEN YOU WANT TO PROTECT YOUR HEART

SUMMARY

Heart disease is the deadliest killer in the United States, so it's crucial to look after your heart. However, even if you've taken what you think is every measure possible, heart disease is still a possibility. Obviously, your heart works hard and is crucial to many of your bodily functions. The thing with heart disease is that we don't know exactly what causes it to begin with, but we do have some pretty good guesses.

High blood pressure, high blood sugar, smoking and inflammation all seem to be linked to heart problems. We have also discovered that certain animal products, particularly eggs and meat, can contain many substances which your gut bacteria metabolizes into things which can cause a lot of damage to your arteries. Even plaques that appear when you're a kid can affect your arteries, which—in turn—is detrimental to a healthy heart. These can also impact other areas of the body, including your skin; this is often why wrinkles are the first indication of arterial aging.

The plagues increase once you reach your thirties and can begin negatively impacting your blood flow. This is obviously a problem. Your heart needs to pump blood through your body, and when it can't, you can have a heart attack.

While heart disease is heavily linked to genetics, it can also stem from lifestyle choices. Depending on your lifestyle changes—such as if you're a regular smoker, your genetics, blood pressure, and blood sugar—you may need to make additional adjustments to your diet.

The When Way Diet recommends a Mediterranean diet, which will help reduce the risk of heart disease for the average person. If you are, however, at a higher than usual risk for heart disease, you also need to cut down the amount of fat you're consuming. While it's an oversimplification to never eat fat, it is something you need to watch if you already are at higher than average risk for heart disease; in this case, avoid eating meat, eggs, and dairy. You may also take a mixed approach with these diets. Eat the When Way Diet for a few weeks, and then, cut down fat for a few. Alternate between the two.

Recap of chapter 33

1. While the risk of heart disease is linked heavily to genetics, heart disease can happen to anyone.
2. A way of lessening the risk of heart disease is in following the When Way.
3. If you are at a higher risk for heart disease—from genetics, a history of smoking, etc.—you need to further cut down on fat in order to lessen your risks.

CHAPTER 34: WHEN YOU NEED TO FORTIFY YOUR SKELETON

SUMMARY

As we get older, we pay more attention to our skeleton. We notice how certain movements hurt, usually because of our muscles or with our joints. Our bodies simply do not work like they used to. Because movement is a complicated process that involves several parts of our body working together in various ways, problems with any single part of our bodies can make these movements more difficult.

One part of our body that we need to consider is our cartilage, which helps our body move. It's important to keep this part of our body hydrated, something which can be helped with avocado and soybean oils; the downside is that you have to extract these oils. Simply eating avocado toast or soybeans won't help, but you can try supplements with these oils in them.

While bones hold us up and protect our organs, they also help produce blood and stem cells. While bones are dense, they do not have a solid structure; it's more like a honeycomb, and if this structure is damaged, it makes your bones weaker and more prone to breaks. Breaks can cause other problems in our bodies; fortunately, we can help fortify our bones by taking in a lot of vitamin D.

Our joints often cause more problems than our bones. The soft cushioning between our bones can deteriorate and result in our bones grinding painfully together. Fortunately, eating the When Way will help control weight and inflammation, two things which can cause this deterioration.

MVPs

While milk does contain calcium, vitamin D, and vitamin K, leafy green vegetables and salmon are better choices for getting these crucial vitamins to promote both bone and joint health. Potassium and magnesium are also good for promoting healthy bones and joints. Furthermore, healthy fats and foods with polyphenols—coffee, avocados, walnuts, and tomatoes—can help keep inflammation at bay. Just be sure to cut the classic sandwich with white bread and processed meats. Instead, opt for whole grains with fish, avocado, or chicken breast.

<u>Recap of chapter 34</u>

1. To build strong bones, you may take soybean or avocado oil supplements.
2. Taking an appropriate amount of vitamin D is a good way to get strong bones.
3. For strong bones, skip the milk and opt for leafy greens, healthy fats, and foods with polyphenols.
4. Salmon is an excellent choice for a heart-healthy food.

CHAPTER 35: WHEN YOU DON'T WANT TO LOSE YOUR MIND

SUMMARY

Our brains are very complex and serve a variety of functions. Unfortunately, as Americans age, we begin to experience cognitive problems. This is further complicated by our own lack of knowledge; we are far from knowing everything there is to know about the brain and how it functions. However, we have a few ideas about why our memory declines the older we get. The short answer is that our brains fire neurons, and these build bridges to send messages through our brains. Sometimes, though, these bridges stop working. One reason for this is simply disuse. The other reason is that these bridges can be damaged by outside matter, including food.

The right food works to build these bridges, while the wrong kind of food can make these bridges harder to build. This is not to say, once more, that food is a wonder cure; genetics does play a pretty big role in a lot of this. However, you can look at foods that might help you.

MVP

Eating the When Way is already a good first step because it acts to fortify your whole body. Eating a lot of salmon salads is a good first step to building those neural bridges. Leafy greens also play a pretty important role in building those bridges, and research shows that people who eat leafy greens show significantly lower amounts of decline.

The healthy fats of walnuts are also a good choice for helping build those bridges. Looking at when you eat and shortening that window of time is yet another way to help build those bridges. As for what to cut, sugar. Processed foods are the worst thing you can eat for encouraging those bridges to build.

Recap of chapter 35

1. To help prevent cognitive decline, it's good to eat the When Way.
2. Eating salmon and a lot of leafy greens is another way to prevent cognitive decline as you age.
3. Walnuts have healthy fats which will foster cognitive growth.
4. Cut out sugars and processed foods, which make it more difficult for your brain to function.

CHAPTER 36: WHEN YOU WANT TO PREVENT TYPE 2 DIABETES

SUMMARY

Part of the reason our country is facing an obesity epidemic is because of our change in diets and the availability of processed food. Weight gain and obesity result in many detrimental conditions, and among them is type 2 diabetes, which stems from an elevated blood glucose caused by resistance to insulin. Type 2 diabetes has a host of problems with it, including damage to eyes, nerves, and kidneys. However, it also causes damage to our heart and brain.

One sure-fire way to prevent diabetes is to lose extra weight and eat healthy foods. Losing weight reduces insulin resistance, and eating better quality foods results in reducing extra sugar and saturated fat that must be processed by your body. Exercise is also crucial, and some research suggests that exercise and a healthy diet may actually be more effective than medication in fighting diabetes. Obviously, the When Way is the best overall approach for fighting diabetes because it involves eating healthy food and maintaining a good weight. However, you can also give yourself a little extra push if you need to.

While we aren't entirely sure why it works, we know that drinking a few cups of coffee regularly reduces the risk of you getting diabetes. Mind you; this only applies if you don't weigh the coffee down with a ton of cream and sugar. Instead, you can try substituting cinnamon and almond milk as sweeteners.

As usual, healthy fats and grains are a must, but polyunsaturated fats—which come from olive oil, avocadoes, and wal-nuts—are also valuable in combatting diabetes. Whole grain and fiber also have this effect. These should already be a staple in your diet, and once more, you want to cut out processed food and red meat. Also, avoid foods which contain simple sugars.

Recap of chapter 36

1. Following the When Way, resulting in a healthy weight and diet, is a sure-fire way of avoiding diabetes.
2. For additional assurance, exercise offers an effective approach.
3. Coffee helps prevent diabetes, provided you don't load it down with creamer and sugar.
4. Polyunsaturated fats are also a good way to lessen the risk of diabetes.

CHAPTER 37: WHEN YOU WANT HEALTHY LUNGS

SUMMARY

Obviously, the first thing you should do if you want healthy lungs is to kick the cigarettes to the curb; everyone knows that. A lot about the health of your lungs is influenced by your environment, though. The bad news is that this means we inhale any number of harmful toxins; the good news is that you can exercise and practice deep breathing techniques, both of which help your lungs. However, you can also pick certain foods that will help you with this endeavor.

MVP

Water is your best friend. Obviously, water aids in hydration, but it also keeps blood flowing to and from your lungs. Water shoulder already be your first choice when it comes to staying hydrated, but it also can't be beat when it comes to lung health.

If you like spices, you're in luck because many spices reduce inflammation. Inflammation can lead to free radicals, which can impair your ability to breathe properly. However, spices lessen inflammation and therefore, lessen the chances of this happening. Specifically, garlic, onions, and turmeric are very good at this. Ginger is also an excellent choice, and research indicates people who also add in a couple of tomatoes are less likely to have difficulties with their lung functions.

Cut out the fried foods. If you're following the When Way, you won't be eating many of these anyway, but fried foods can add fat, which can make it harder to breathe. For healthy eating, consider substituting pretzels with celery sticks, corn with cabbage or cauliflower, a bite-size piece of candy with an apple, and carbonated drinks with water.

Recap of chapter 37

1. When trying to build healthy lungs, hydration is key, so drink a lot of water.
2. Spices are great for preventing inflammation, which in turn, helps your lungs function unimpaired.
3. Do away with fried foods, which can cause a build-up of fat and result in it being harder to breathe.

CHAPTER 38: WHEN YOU WANT TO REDUCE INFLAMMATION

SUMMARY

We know that inflammation is not a good thing, but you may not entirely know what inflammation does to your body. And yet understanding inflammation is critically important. At its most basic level, inflammation is good. It tells your body when there's something wrong, such as when you have a cold or allergic reaction. The body identifies something wrong and works to fix it. Your immune cells work to fight the invader, sometimes resulting in inflammation. But if you develop chronic inflammation, this is not a good thing. Your body is constantly fighting, and this is a problem that builds. This is specifically a problem that builds when you eat too much animal protein or saturated fat.

Because inflammation is a natural response, you obviously need it, but it's important to keep it in check and not make your body work overtime. There is, of course, the usual list of things you shouldn't do in order to prevent inflammation. You should avoid smoking and eating processes foods—including meats.

When You Eat

When you move, your body slows down inflammation; when you slow down, inflammation speeds up. This is why it's an especially bad idea to eat inflammatory foods before you go to bed. Inflammation can be heightened while you're sleeping. Eating while you're very stressed can have a similar effect, also.

What You Eat

If you're following the When Way, you're already eating a lot of anti-inflammatory foods. Fruits, vegetables, and healthy fats are the best food sources for fighting overactive inflammation. More specifically, you want to eat a lot of vitamin C and prebiotic fiber. You also want to eat a lot of fish and nuts, with a bit of extra virgin olive oil thrown in the mix. Greek and Icelandic yogurt are also good options because they contain good bacteria that helps your gut. Finally, oats will slow the inflammation process. Of course, you also should avoid sugars, syrups, saturated and trans fat, and egg yolks.

Recap of chapter 38

1. Inflammation is a natural process in our body; however, it can become too much and cause us pain, particularly if we're leading an unhealthy lifestyle.

2. To prevent problems with inflammation, make sure you're eating the When Way and not eating inflammatory foods, especially before going to bed at night.

3. Fruits, vegetables, and healthy fats are the best way to prevent problems with inflammation.

CHAPTER 39: WHEN YOU HAVE HORMONAL ISSUES

SUMMARY

Our bodies are intricate ecosystems that are dependent on numerous factors to function properly and to their full potential. Hormones are a part of this system, and they're incredibly complicated. Some people have abnormal hormonal systems, which may require medication and treatments. These are vast and numerous, but it's also worth noting that some hormonal problems can be managed or eliminated with proper diets.

Hormonal glands play an important role in almost every function of our bodies, but the problem is that it's difficult to figure hormones out. Tests can, for example, show levels of hormones, but not every hormonal level works for every single person. As for food's relationship to hormones, it depends specifically on which hormone is being discussed.

Thyroid

The thyroid's hormones are associates with symptoms such as weight management, heart rate, and more. These can be both hyperactive and underactive, and either one can wreak havoc on your body. Hyperthyroidism, the overactive thyroid, can result in organ damage, heart disease, and eye disease. Fortunately, this can be managed by following the When Way. Eat plenty of plant-based protein including leafy greens and cruciferous vegetables, which will protect bones and may help with your hyperthyroid. You might also need to cut back on iodine, so consult with your doctor.

Hypothyroidism, the underactive thyroid, requires a lot of iodine to kick it back into gear. Low-mercury fish and iodized salt are lifesavers. You might also help your thyroid if you avoid nitrates, a substance found commonly in processed meats. If you happen to be taking hormones for your hypothyroid, do not mix them with soy, as soy may prevent your hormones from absorbing properly. So save the soy milk for a little while after you've taken your hormones.

Adrenal

These hormones regulate many bodily functions such as energy, blood pressure, and digestion among others. This hormone also controls your stress response, so it's crucial to ensure its functioning properly. The best way to manage stress is not to eat. Instead, try another approach for managing your stress. This is because stress eating can easily lead to fat, which is all-around a bad idea.

Skin

For healthy skin, make sure you're getting an appropriate dose of vitamin D. There are many ways to get this, but good ones include salmon and leafy greens.

Recap of chapter 39

1. Managing hormones depends on which hormone is being discussed.
2. For an overactive thyroid, eat plenty of leafy greens and cruciferous vegetables, which will protect bones and may help manage your thyroid.
3. For an underactive thyroid, low-mercury fish and iodized salt can't be beat.
4. Avoid stress eating to keep your adrenal (and your waistline) in good shape.
5. For healthy skin, eat lots of vitamin D.

CHAPTER 40: WHEN YOU HAVE OTHER HEALTH ISSUES

SUMMARY

There are many other health issues that you may have, and many of them require a holistic approach. Food alone is crucial but not enough. Often, a healthy diet must be accompanied by exercise, stress management, or other interventions. But we do still need to consider food and how it may help with our various ailments. Thus, we have a few recommendations for common ailments you may encounter.

Cataracts

Cataracts can be removed with surgery. However, choosing certain foods can help prevent them from ever forming to begin with. Polyunsaturated fats, protein, vitamins A, C, and E, along with numerous other minerals are shown to help prevent cataracts. This is, again, where salmon and spinach come in handy. Research also links an increased risk of cataracts to people with carb-heavy diets.

Gallstones

Gallstones are hard stones that form in you digestive system and cause a lot of pain to your gallbladder, bringing with them the heightened risk for infection. Simply following the When Way will greatly reduce your risk for these, but moderating caffeine, alcohol, and nuts is also a good way to lower the risk for these. High fiber diets serve as an additional deterrent.

Gout

Gout is a type of arthritis commonly associated for flaring up in your big toe. A good way to lower the chances of getting gout is to have a diet composed of the three macronutrients and to drink lots of water. Avoiding foods containing purines is also a definite step to take; the one exception is when purines are in fruits and vegetables, such as peas.

Kidney Stones

Kidney stones are incredibly painful, as you may have heard. The best way to prevent these is deceptively simply; drink a lot of water and stay hydrated. You can also make sure you're getting plenty of calcium.

Restless Leg Syndrome

This can really wreak havoc on your sleeping schedule. The best way to help this is by making sure you're eating fish and spinach; you might be deficient in certain vitamins. This may also be an indication of a more serious problem. Try cutting out red meat, adding folate and magnesium. Also, avoid caffeine and alcohol before bed, as these can be detrimental to your sleep schedule.

Recap of chapter 40

1. Many additional problems can be solved simply by eating the When Way.

2. To lessen the risk of cataracts, eat polyunsaturated fats, protein, vitamins A, C, and E, along with much-needed minerals.

3. Gallstones can be deterred by moderating caffeine, alcohol, and nuts.

4. Hydration and avoiding purines in meat both serve as good deterrents for gout.

5. Hydration and sufficient calcium can lessen your risk for getting kidney stones.

6. Restless leg syndrome can be eased by getting enough nutrients and avoiding caffeine and alcohol before bedtime.

PART 4: THE FINAL WORD: WHAT TO EAT WHEN

CHAPTER 41: HOW TO WIN
THE WHEN WAY

SUMMARY

It is entirely reasonable to be tempted by food that doesn't follow the When Way. We are bombarded constantly by fast food, packaged food, and chocolate at check-out. Keep in mind that temptation isn't your fault. We are hardwired to want sugar and fat. This, obviously, does not mean that you should binge-eat an entire carton of ice cream in one setting, but understanding that eating is your gut instinct will allow you to think more carefully about your impulse buys.

Part of the problem with our diet in America is the food industry. They have made it much harder to eat healthy, and they've done this by processing food and packing it full of sugar. Thus, giving into temptation is made worse than it normally might have been, had the food industry—say—not filled those healthy-sounding granola bars with a ton of sugar.

Don't think of eating healthy as being about willpower. It's instead about forming a strategy and preparing ahead to better combat temptation when it rears its head.

You should also focus on creating an environment that helps you make smart choices. For example, if your morning stop involves buying a dozen donuts on the way to work, keep healthy When Way snacks on hand to curb cravings, and above all, plan your meals ahead. If you know you're going out to happy hour after work, eat before you go to help curb your cravings.

Recap of chapter 41

1. It's okay to be tempted by food; just think through your impulse buys.
2. The food industry is partly to blame for our eating problems.
3. Think of eating the When Way as being strategic rather than a matter of willpower.
4. Create environments that support healthy eating habits.

IMPORTANT FACTS RECAP

Recap- Chapter 1: The Science of When: When You Eat Is Just as Important as What You Eat

1. To eat healthy, looking at *when* we eat is just as important as *what* we eat.
2. Our body has a natural rhythm, our circadian clock, that we must align with our internal food clock.
3. For best results, we should eat more early in that day rather than later.

Recap- Chapter 2: A Nutritious Breakdown: Understand the Building Blocks of Your Diet

1. Our bodies require three macronutrients—carbohydrates, fats, and proteins—to function.
2. The key to being healthy is to know the effects that macronutrients have on our body; all these macronutrients are crucial to our health, but too much of any one can have adverse effects.
3. Unhealthy eating can cause the gain of dangerous visceral fat, which can be lost by mastering *when* to eat.

Recap- Chapter 3: Time to Eat!: Four Guidelines for Setting Your Food Clock

1. Eat during the day, mostly during a consistent twelve-hour window.

2. Front-load the majority of your calories for the morning and eat less at night.

3. Eat consistently from day-to-day.

4. Don't stereotype certain types of food as belonging to a certain meal (i.e. eggs for breakfast or a feast at dinner) and eat when is most *beneficial* to you.

Recap- Chapter 4: The When Way: A 31-Day Plan

1. You do not have to become a healthy eating guru overnight; instead, keep track of your progress and slowly work towards better eating over a month-long period.

2. Work towards incorporating more leafy greens, healthy fats, and whole grains and less processed foods, unhealthy fats, starchy vegetables, and sugary desserts.

3. Eliminate those late night snacks.

Recap- Chapter 5: Food for Thought: Mindful Eating for More Majestic Meals

1. We should focus on eating mindfully and slowing down.

2. Remember to consider the place when you eat, choosing a place that is calm and free of stressful distractions.

3. Take the time to taste and smell your food. Enjoy it.

Recap- Chapter 6: What to Eat...When You're Stressed and Hangry

1. While it is tempting to eat junk when we're stressed, we should try our best not to.

2. When we're stressed, we're more susceptible to wanting fast food, so it's best to try and steer our commutes away from fast food places.

3. It doesn't hurt, though, to keep an emergency stash of healthy foods—such as roasted chickpeas or butter-free popcorn—on hand to help us when we have the impulse to eat out of stress.

Recap- Chapter 7: What to Eat...When You're Feeling Fatigued

1. Drinking the appropriate amount of water is key in helping combat fatigue.

2. We can also beat fatigue by beginning our days right and front-loading with healthy, unsaturated fats and proteins.

3. Coffee and tea might help us get through the day, and these are good choices—provided they aren't loaded up with creams, sugars, and syrups.

Recap- Chapter 8: What to Eat...When You're Bummed

1. While our first instinct may be to eat a lot of sugar when we're sad, this is not a good idea.

2. Instead, healthy carbohydrates—such as peanut butter

toast—are a good way to lighten our mood.

3. In the long-term, fish and green tea can't be beat for kicking away our blues.

Recap- Chapter 9: What to Eat…When You're Grieving

1. When you're grieving, accept help, and if family members offer to make you food, don't hesitate to tell them what you like.

2. If you are too emotionally exhausted to make a full trip to the grocery store, use the express lane or have a friend or loved one make the trip for you.

3. Establish a routine with what you eat; routines, while normally boring, will only help you when you're grieving.

Recap- Chapter 10: What to Eat…When You Cannot Sleep

1. Sleep is crucial for being healthy because our bodies repair themselves when we're sleeping.

2. Eating foods that contain magnesium and tryptophan can help encourage better quality sleep.

3. Eating fiber-rich desserts is a good way of curbing the desire for less healthy midnight snacks.

Recap- Chapter 11: What to Eat...When You Get Headaches a Lot

1. Headaches have many causes and many cures and are not a one-size-fits-all.
2. Keeping track of foods that may trigger headaches and switching them out with other foods may lessen the number of headaches you have.
3. Headaches are also often the result of a lack of magnesium, so eating magnesium-rich foods may also help lessen them.

Recap- Chapter 12: What to Eat...When You're Sick

1. It's important to eat good food, with nutrients such a vitamin C, to help us prevent getting sick.
2. When we are sick, chicken soup, garlic, ginger, and mushrooms can help us get well quickly.
3. When we're sick, we also want to eat wisely in order to compensate for our compromised immune systems by replacing certain foods—orange juice for oranges, sushi for cooked salmon or trout, and chia seeds with water-logged oatmeal.

Recap- Chapter 13: What to Eat...When You're in Pain

1. If you are in chronic pain, you should have physical therapy to help you better manage it.
2. Pain is not inherently bad; it tells us when we need to

make changes.

3. To lessen inflammation and pain, we should eat Mediterranean based diets including olive oil and walnuts.

4. Spicy foods and ginger are also good for preventing inflammation.

5. In order to manage pain, we should cut out sugary foods and carbs, which will help our body feel better in the long-term.

Recap- Chapter 14: What to Eat...When You Have Digestive Problems

1. There are many reasons we might have digestive problems.

2. When you have diarrhea and vomiting, it's important to stay hydrated and eat the BRAT (bananas, rice, apples, and toast) diet.

3. Constipation can be lessened by eating the CRAP (cranberries, raisins, apricots, and prunes) diet.

4. Reflux can be managed by altering the foods you eat, specifically by cutting out spicy food along with caffeine and alcohol.

5. Bloating can be lessened by eating more slowly and opting for slow-digesting carbohydrates.

Recap- Chapter 15: What to Eat…When You're Being Tested

1. Tea and coffee are ideal drinks for when you need to focus on any important mental task.
2. Slow digesting carbohydrates are also good for keeping focused.
3. Resist anything you find in the vending machine; it might help you in the short-term, but the sudden burst of energy will quickly crash.

Recap- Chapter 16: What to Eat…When You Have a Job Interview

1. The morning of an important interview, it's a good idea to begin with whole grains, perhaps, with added flax.
2. Eat a meal ninety minutes before your interview, preferably one that includes the three macronutrients.
3. A cup or two of coffee might be helpful for improving alertness during interviews.
4. Take a bottle of water with you to your interview, to prevent your throat from drying out but also to help increase your alertness.

Recap- Chapter 17: What to Eat…When You Have to Make an Important Decision

1. Many factors can influence us when we make decisions.
2. To make good decisions, we should be sure we're getting

enough sleep, which is more likely if we're eating the When Way.

3. Eating foods rich in omega-3 oils as well as drinking reasonable amounts of coffee and tea can help us think clearly and make better decisions.

Recap- Chapter 18: What to Eat...When You're on the Go

1. If you have to eat on the go, eat wisely.
2. Eat nuts, packs of sliced fruit, Greek yogurt, and hummus; drink water, coffee, or tea if you're in a pinch.
3. Be careful with healthy-sounding foods like granola bars and trail mix; these can have a lot of hidden sugar.

Recap- Chapter 19: What to Eat...When You Have an Event

1. When attending a work function that involves food, eat a couple of apples beforehand, to minimize the desire to eat everything and anything.
2. Drink water and/or coffee, both for hydration and to keep your hands busy, cutting back on mindless eating.
3. If you're attending a work function with a buffet, look over everything before choosing something to eat; this will help you keep from overeating everything.

Recap- Chapter 20: What to Eat...When You're on Vacation

1. It's okay to indulge a little on vacation, but don't go overboard.
2. Strategies such as splitting meals, substituting for healthier sides, arranging your eating into your schedule, paying attention to sides, and staying hydrated can help you stay on track while on vacation.
3. Remember that you don't have to clear your plate at every single meal; you can try new things without over-indulging.

Recap- Chapter 21: What to Eat...When It's the Holiday Season

1. During the holidays, it's okay to indulge a little bit, but don't go overboard.
2. Drinking water during holiday parties is a good way to keep yourself from overeating or from drinking to many alcohol beverages.
3. If you are going to indulge a bit, try to avoid desserts including saturated fat and partially hydrogenated oils.
4. Skip the self-basting turkeys and opt for basting yourself with homemade or pre-made, low sodium broth.

Recap- Chapter 22: What to Eat...When You're at the Stadium

1. Instead of going for the first fried food you find, bring healthy snacks if you can.
2. If you do eat at the stadium, peanuts are the best option by far, but turkey sausage and grilled chicken sandwiches sans bun are also good options.
3. Keep the usual, stereotypical stadium foods—such as nachos, sodas, etc.—to a minimum.

Recap- Chapter 23: What to Eat...When You're on a Date

1. A good first date should include salad, although make sure to avoid the unhealthy dressings.
2. If you're ordering food with marinara, have it on the side.
3. Dark chocolate is a good food for reducing anxiety.
4. So-called aphrodisiacs—oysters, dark chocolate, and avocados—have no basis in science, but they're still healthy foods to consider.
5. For meals before the date, look at foods which release energy slowly.

Recap- Chapter 24: What to Eat...When You Exercise

1. Exercise if crucial for living a healthy lifestyle.
2. For best results, you usually want to eat before rather than after a workout.
3. Experiment with your diet for best results.

4. Grilled chicken, black beans, and sweet potatoes are excellent foods for keeping your muscles healthy after exercise.

5. Try to resist the sweet siren's call of eating too many sugary rewards for exercising.

Recap- Chapter 25: What to Eat...When You're Trying to Become Pregnant (Or Already Are)

1. While fertility depends on many factors, many of the factors that might cause infertility, like stress, can be combated with proper, healthy eating.

2. When pregnant, grilled salmon salad is a perfect source of nutrients for you and your growing child.

3. When pregnant, avoid high-mercury fish like tuna.

4. Increase your dairy intake, but keep an eye on the amount of fat you're consuming; consider opting for Greek or Icelandic yogurt as good dairy alternatives.

Recap- Chapter 26: What to Eat...When You're Nursing

1. When breastfeeding, it's important to remember that your baby is consuming that same foods that you are.

2. Breast milk contains both the three macronutrients as well as much-needed vitamins to your baby, but it is not the only option; formula and a combination of formula and breastmilk also provide needed nutrients to your baby.

3. Salmon or ocean trout are good foods to eat, as they contain healthy omega-3 oils.
4. Zinc is also important when breastfeeding.
5. When breastfeeding, it's important to avoid foods that are uncooked or high at risk for containing mercury, such as tuna.

Recap- Chapter 27: What to Eat...When You Have PMS or Period Pain

1. When on your period, hydration is key to preventing bloating.
2. Dark chocolate can help you manage stress and curb cravings for other, less healthy foods during your period.
3. If you have a rough time during your period, try cutting out caffeine and alcohol, as these can often worse symptoms.

Recap- Chapter 28: What to Eat...When You Have Hot Flashes

1. Hot flashes are caused by our changing levels of estrogen as we get older.
2. Eating soybeans and a Mediterranean diet can help lessen the amount of hot flashes you experience.
3. Cutting out caffeine can also lessen the number of hot flashes you have.

Recap- Chapter 29: What to Eat...When You Need a Testosterone Boost

1. Testosterone is a varied hormone with many functions.
2. While many testosterone supplements exist, these are not necessarily the best choice for a long-term increase in your testosterone levels.
3. Eating fruit salads (of pomegranates, grapes, and watermelon), cabbage sprinkled with pumpkin seeds, and salmon are good foods to eat if your goal is to improve testosterone levels.

Recap- Chapter 30: What to Eat...When You Want to Improve Fertility

1. There are many factors that may increase or decrease fertility, but one that can be helped through proper diet is sperm quality.
2. Walnuts and fish, and lots of them, are the best choices for improving sperm quality and quantity.
3. Tomatoes are also important, as they appear to boost sperm quality.
4. Skip out on the red meat and dairy, which lower semen quality.

Recap- Chapter 31: What to Eat...When You Need to Shrink Your Prostate

1. If you notice problems with urinating or with your penis functioning properly, it is a good idea to talk to a medical professional.
2. Zinc is crucial for a healthy prostate, and eating spinach is a good way of getting it.
3. Nuts, seeds, and beans are good for encouraging prostate health.
4. If you do have an enlarged prostate, cut out caffeine, which can worsen the symptoms of it.

Recap- Chapter 32: What to Eat...When You Have a History of Cancer

1. Even small changes like exercise and eating the When Way can help minimize your risk of cancer.
2. A good immune system, built by taking in vitamin D, is also crucial in lessening the risk of cancer.
3. Eating antioxidants, found often in berries, is a good way to lessen the risk of free radicals, another way cancer forms.
4. Coffee and tea may also help prevent cancer.
5. Cut out red meat to lessen a risk of cancer.

Recap- Chapter 33: What to Eat...When You Want to Protect Your Heart

1. While the risk of heart disease is linked heavily to genetics, heart disease can happen to anyone.
2. A way of lessening the risk of heart disease is in following the When Way.
3. If you are at a higher risk for heart disease—from genetics, a history of smoking, etc.—you need to further cut down on fat in order to lessen your risks.

Recap- Chapter 34: What to Eat...When You Need to Fortify Your Skeleton

1. To build strong bones, you may take soybean or avocado oil supplements.
2. Taking an appropriate amount of vitamin D is a good way to get strong bones.
3. For strong bones, skip the milk and opt for leafy greens, healthy fats, and foods with polyphenols.
4. Salmon is an excellent choice for a heart-healthy food.

Recap- Chapter 35: What to Eat...When You Want to Keep from Losing Your Mind

1. To help prevent cognitive decline, it's good to eat the When Way.
2. Eating salmon and a lot of leafy greens is another way to prevent cognitive decline as you age.

3. Walnuts have healthy fats which will foster cognitive growth.
4. Cut out sugars and processed foods, which make it more difficult for your brain to function.

Recap- Chapter 36: What to Eat...When You Want to Avoid Type 2 Diabetes

1. Following the When Way, resulting in a healthy weight and diet, is a sure-fire way of avoiding diabetes.
2. For additional assurance, exercise offers an effective approach.
3. Coffee helps prevent diabetes, provided you don't load it down with creamer and sugar.
4. Polyunsaturated fats are also a good way to lessen the risk of diabetes.

Recap- Chapter 37: What to Eat...When You Want Healthy Lungs

1. When trying to build healthy lungs, hydration is key, so drink a lot of water.
2. Spices are great for preventing inflammation, which in turn, helps your lungs function unimpaired.
3. Do away with fried foods, which can cause a build-up of fat and result in it being harder to breathe.

Recap- Chapter 38: What to Eat...When You Want to Reduce Inflammation

1. Inflammation is a natural process in our body; however, it can become too much and cause us pain, particularly if we're leading an unhealthy lifestyle.
2. To prevent problems with inflammation, make sure you're eating the When Way and not eating inflammatory foods, especially before going to bed at night.
3. Fruits, vegetables, and healthy fats are the best way to prevent problems with inflammation.

Recap- Chapter 39: What to Eat...When You Have Hormonal Issues

1. Managing hormones depends on which hormone is being discussed.
2. For an overactive thyroid, eat plenty of leafy greens and cruciferous vegetables, which will protect bones and may help manage your thyroid.
3. For an underactive thyroid, low-mercury fish and iodized salt can't be beat.
4. Avoid stress eating to keep your adrenal (and your waistline) in good shape.
5. For healthy skin, eat lots of vitamin D.

Recap- Chapter 40: What to Eat...When You Have Other Health Issues

1. Many additional problems can be solved simply by eating the When Way.

2. To lessen the risk of cataracts, eat polyunsaturated fats, protein, vitamins A, C, and E, along with much-needed minerals.

3. Gallstones can be deterred by moderating caffeine, alcohol, and nuts.

4. Hydration and avoiding purines in meat both serve as good deterrents for gout.

5. Hydration and sufficient calcium can lessen your risk for getting kidney stones.

6. Restless leg syndrome can be eased by getting enough nutrients and avoiding caffeine and alcohol before bedtime.

Recap- Chapter 41: How to Win the When Way— Managing Temptation

1. It's okay to be tempted by food; just think through your impulse buys.

2. The food industry is partly to blame for our eating problems.

3. Think of eating the When Way as being strategic rather than a matter of willpower.

4. Create environments that support healthy eating habits.

ANALYSIS & ACTION PLAN

Overall, *What to Eat When* presents a vast, informative guide for what to eat and when. This multi-faceted approach addresses the when aspect by encouraging readers to eat more in the morning and less at night, which results in this book standing out far more than many others you might find in the bookstore. It's more than a checklist of what to eat and what not to eat. Instead, it's an entirely different lifestyle that accommodates a variety of situations that we might find ourselves in. It's a roadmap for navigating our own health.

Ultimately, the When Way can be summed up with the ten rules that are stated in its conclusion. These are as follows: 1.) eat when the sun is out; 2.) eat more early in the day, less later; 3.) stop stereotyping foods; 4.) balance your nutrients; 5.) realize that you can eat well in any situation; 6.) don't let mistakes derail you; 7.) be social; 8.) stay hydrated; 9.) make a plan; and 10.) love what you eat. When implementing the When Way, it wouldn't hurt to list these out and hang them on your refrigerator. Trying to begin a new dieting plan can be intimidating, particularly when there are so many different variables and foods to consider. Make your list and work on making small changes over the period of a month or longer. Keep in mind that you should be kind to yourself, and self-improvement is always a good goal. You don't have to turn your entire life around in one day, though.

As you're looking at the long-term, consider what foods pop up repeatedly in the When Way. Salmon, for example, seems to pop up over and over again. Look for foods that show up frequently that you like or think you might like and slowly find ways to incorporate them into your diet while slowly eating more earlier in the day and working to cut out unneeded foods. Remember to keep your goals realistic as you're setting out and doing this. If you can manage to start an entirely different dietary plan, a new exercise regimen, and shift the time you eat all your meals in a single day, your strategic planning is admirable; however, if you can't tackle all of that at once, there's no shame in that either. If you need to introduce these changes gradually, do that. Any improvement is better than none at all, and if you make mistakes, brush them off and try again.

DISCUSSION QUESTIONS TO GET YOU THINKING

1. Eating the When Way involves much more than simply eating at a certain time of day. What else does eating the When Way involve?

2. Many foods in the When Way appear over and over in a variety of situations. Can you remember what they are?

3. Aside from food, what else does the When Way recommend for a healthy lifestyle?

4. How does the When Way meet or challenge your expectations for a dietary plan?

5. Who do you think the When Way would be best suited for?

6. What does the When Way say about temptation?

7. What aspect of the When Way would be the easiest to implement and why? What about the hardest aspect?

8. What foods surprised you when learning about the When Way?

9. Plan your meals for a single day following the When Way. What meals did you choose and why?

10. We are generally very busy in our daily lives. What are some ways we can slow down, and how might this impact what we eat?

ABOUT HIGH SPEED READS

Here at High Speed Reads our goal is to save you time by providing the best summaries possible. We stand out from our competitors by not only including all of the pertinent facts from the subject book but also a personal analysis of the book with action plan, easy to follow summaries of each chapter including a list of chapter highlights, a thirty second summary of the entire book and even discussion questions to get you thinking.

As you can see we go above and beyond to make your purchase a pleasant one. If you learned something beneficial from this book please leave a positive review so others can benefit as well. Lastly if you haven't yet make sure you purchase the subject book, What to Eat When, by visiting
https://amzn.to/2TZn5n2